Vaughan Public Libraries
2191 Major Mackenzie Dr.
Maple, Ontario
905-653-READ (7323)

D0566984

J 398.45 Redmo

Redmond, S.
Mermaids.

MERMAIDS

SHIRLEY RAYE REDMOND

KIDHAVEN PRESS
A part of Gale, Cengage Learning

GALE
CENGAGE Learning·

Detroit • New York • San Francisco • New Haven, Conn • Waterville, Maine • London

GALE
CENGAGE Learning·

© 2008 Gale, Cengage Learning

For more information, contact
KidHaven Press
27500 Drake Rd.
Farmington Hills, MI 48331-3535
Or you can visit our Internet site at gale.cengage.com

ALL RIGHTS RESERVED.
No part of this work covered by the copyright hereon may be reproduced or used in any form or by any means—graphic, electronic, or mechanical, including photocopying, recording, taping, Web distribution or information storage retrieval systems—without the written permission of the publisher.

Every effort has been made to trace the owners of copyrighted material.

LIBRARY OF CONGRESS CATALOGING-IN-PUBLICATION DATA

Redmond, Shirley-Raye, 1955-
  Mermaids / by Shirley Raye Redmond.
    p. cm. -- (Monsters)
  Includes bibliographical references and index.
  ISBN 978-0-7377-3634-2 (hardcover)
  1. Mermaids--Juvenile literature. I. Title.
  GR910.R43 2008
  398'.45--dc22

                                                                    2007021293

ISBN-10: 0-7377-3634-8

Printed in the United States of America
2 3 4 5 6 7 12 11 10 09 08

CONTENTS

CHAPTER 1

SAILOR, BEWARE!

For thousands of years, seamen told fantastic tales about mysterious creatures, such as sea serpents, giant squid, and other monsters of the deep. But none have captured the imagination as much as the fascinating stories of mysterious mermaids. Mermaids and mermen are fabled creatures who live in water—both freshwater and saltwater. The word "mere" is an old English word for "sea."

Often seen wearing a red cap, the mermaid has the head and upper body of a woman. From the waist down, she is a fish. Instead of legs, she has the scaly body of a fish and the **flukes** of a dolphin.

Opposite: It seems that no other sea creature has captured the imagination more than the mermaid.

Lamias are creatures similar to mermaids. They are also beautiful women from the waist up. But, instead of a body like a fish, they have the coiling body of an eel or water snake. They speak with a gentle, pleasing hiss. Lamias entice their victims to come near and when they do, they eat them! Some say lamias also drink the blood of children. Like lamias, mermaids are a symbol of death and doom. They are heartless and have no pity for the sailors and boatmen they lure to their watery graves.

Origins

Nearly all countries in the world have tales of water creatures that are half-human and half-fish. One of the most ancient tales is about a Babylonian man-fish god named Oannes, who lived in the sea. Accounts of Oannes date back to 5000 or 4000 B.C. He shed his scaly fish tail each morning and spent all day on land. In the evening, as the sun sank low on the horizon, Oannes returned to the sea. Oannes was worshipped for being the giver of knowledge. He could also see into the future and tell what was going to happen before it took place.

Oannes's female counterpart was called Atargatis, a **fertility** goddess. Atargatis is often compared to the Greek goddess, Aphrodite, and the Roman goddess, Venus. According to myth, Atargatis was once entirely human. She murdered her lover, abandoned her baby, and then threw herself into the sea. But she did not drown. Instead, she became half-woman and half-fish. Atargatis was beautiful and vain. She was also seductive and cruel. These traits became common to mermaids around the world. Mermaids are also said to be greedy, spiteful, and jealous.

The cruel, dangerous nature of mermaids was commonly accepted in the days of Alexander the Great. Alexander was king of Macedon and one of the most successful military conquerors of all time. One legend tells how he and his men

The mermaid Atargatis is often compared to the Roman goddess Venus, pictured here.

captured two river mermaids. These evil creatures had been tempting men into the river, where they tied their victims with water reeds and tormented the suffering men until they drowned.

Unable to live long out of the water, the captive river mermaids died soon after they were trapped by Alexander and his men. According to the legend, Alexander described them being "as white as snow . . . and they were taller than men have custom to be."[1]

Sailor, Beware!

SOMETHING FISHY

Descriptions of mermaids vary, depending on where they are found. Sometimes, mermaids are quite beautiful, with long golden hair and pearly white skin. One will often be depicted sitting on a rock, holding a mirror in one hand and combing her long wet hair with the other. Nixies are German freshwater mermaids with golden hair and sharp green teeth. Scottish creatures called Fuaths have yellow hair too, but they are not beautiful. They have webbed hands and no noses at all. In Scotland, Ireland, and the Scandinavian countries, some sea people are part human and part seal.

Mermaids are capable of breathing in the water or on land.

The most common image of a mermaid is one of her sitting on a rock and combing her long beautiful hair.

Sailor, Beware!

Other mermaids are described as having blue skin, black or green hair, and pointed teeth. The Shawano Indians of North America have a myth about a merman with green hair and a porpoise face leading the Shawano from Siberia to the North American continent. The Vodyanoi of the Slavic countries in Europe are very frightening. They look like humans with paws and horns. They are covered with grass and moss and are not friendly to humans at all.

Mermaids can breathe equally well in the water and on land. They have a keen sense of hearing, speak multiple languages, and love music. Mermaids are mammals and are said to have reproductive organs similar to dolphins. Like dolphins, mermaid babies are born alive, not hatched from eggs. Mermaids prefer to eat fish and other seafood, but some, such as nixies, lamias, and the *ningyo* of Japan, frequently crave human blood and flesh.

Seeing a mermaid on an ocean voyage—whether she was beautiful or not—was usually considered an unlucky **omen** of impending doom or a terrible storm. It was particularly unlucky when a mermaid tossed a fish onboard the ship. When that happened, sailors warned, one must immediately throw something made of iron—a nail or a horseshoe, for instance—toward the mermaid in the water. It was said that iron took away a mermaid's evil powers.

DEADLY EMBRACE

According to the earliest tales told about them, mermaids are heartless and cruel. A single kiss or passionate embrace usually results in the sailor's death by drowning. There are many tales about enchanted sailors and boatmen who

Many sailors have fallen into the water to their deaths trying to reach in to give a mermaid a kiss.

lean over the sides of their ships or fishing vessels just a little too far, in an attempt to hug or kiss a tempting mermaid. The smiling mermaid then pulls her victim to his watery grave or holds him captive as a slave in her sea cave or keeps him prisoner under a lobster pot.

Brazilian mermaids are said to be particularly fierce. With the strength of a python, a Brazilian mermaid embraces her victim so hard that she crushes him to pieces. After plunging with her prey to the ocean's depth, she takes a bite of his nose, eyes, and other tender body parts, such as the tips of his thumbs and fingers.

A ferocious mermaid attempts to strangle Prince Arthur with her coiling tail in *The Faerie Queene* by Edmund Spenser. Arthur wins the battle when he succeeds in strangling her first. There are numerous Scottish ballads about Macphie of Colonsay, a young man who tried to escape from a pursuing mermaid. His dog jumped into the waves in an attempt to rescue his master. During the deadly fight, Macphie escapes to shore. But his dog and the mermaid kill each other in a snarling fury of sea foam and blood.

In Nigerian folklore, mermaids are fierce but faithful servants of Igbaghon, a river goddess and ruler of the underworld. The mermaids watch for intruders—men and women who bathe or wash their clothes in the goddess's sacred river. The unlucky intruders are then snatched from the riverbank, never to be seen again.

CHAPTER

MERMAIDS AROUND THE WORLD

Mermaid legends and folktales are ancient and widespread. Wherever there are rivers and lakes, oceans and seas, one will find old stories of the water creatures that are half-human and half-fish. The stories have been passed down from one generation to the next. In Japan, mermaids are called ningyo; in Africa, mami wata. The Danish call them maremind and the Dutch use the term "sea-wyf." No matter if they are called kelpies, nixies, tritonids, or water sprites, mermaids are alluring. They also are thought to have supernatural powers.

The Gift of Prophecy

Some say that mermaids can foretell the future. There are many stories about mermaids announcing the arrival of dangerous storms or predicting the sinking of specific ships. According to legend, a mermaid named Isbrandt foretold the birth of King Christian IV of Denmark in 1577. Christian inherited the throne at the age of nine and grew up to be one of the nation's most popular rulers. He supported trade and shipping and was a creative builder. Many of his architectural projects survive to this day.

If you snatch a mermaid's red cap or comb or mirror, you can demand that she tell your fortune or give you gold from the sea. She may even grant you three wishes. But don't demand too much! When angry, mermaids often put a curse on those who waken their rage. Supposedly, this happened to a prosperous port city in Cornwall, England, hundreds of year ago. One of the townsmen took aim at a mermaid, attempting to shoot and capture her. The outraged mermaid cursed the harbor. It filled up with silt and mud, and ships were no longer able to enter the port. This ended the town's busy seaport trade, and the citizens were poverty-stricken.

Opposite: Water sprites, like mermaids, are alluring and are thought to have supernatural powers.

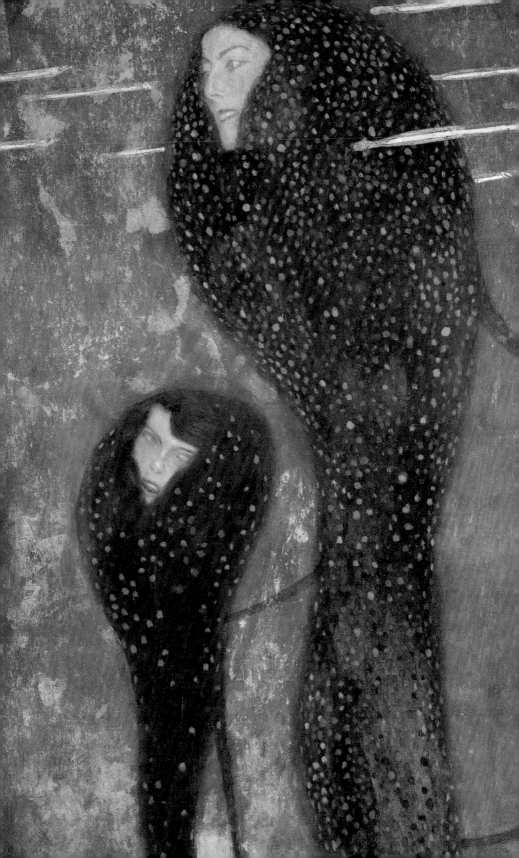

Global Shape-Shifters

Mermaids are capable of **metamorphosis**, or transformation, too. That is, they can change from one shape into other. One of the earliest Greek myths tells how a mermaid named Clytie washed up onto a sandy beach. She became so entranced by the sun, she wouldn't return to the sea. Soon, her scaly fish tail coiled itself down into the sand. Her golden hair turned to petals around her face, and her long fingers became green leaves. She transformed into a Greek sunflower.

Greek citizens surround the former mermaid Clytie who was transformed into a sunflower after becoming entranced with the sun.

Frequently, mermaids would change their fish tails into long, slender legs and walk about on land. Occasionally, one would appear in human form at the village market and was easily identified by her wet apron and red cap.

But not all of the mermaids' shape-shifting is so innocent! Dracs are evil water creatures that live in the rivers of France. They can take the shape of cups or rings floating on the river's surface. When a woman comes to the edge of the riverbank, the Dracs transform back into their original fearful forms. They drag their screaming victim down into the watery depths to enslave her or eat her—and sometimes both!

The Vodyanoi change appearance frequently. They sometimes look old and then young again. They transform themselves from half-naked women to old men with green hair and scraggly beards. Those unlucky enough to be caught in the lake where the Vodyanoi live are drowned or forced to become slaves in the creatures' underwater castles.

SEAL FOLK

In the Scandinavian countries, as well as Ireland and Scotland, sea creatures called *selkies* or *roane* can change from seals into humans on land. Although they are not mermaids, selkies have some similar traits, such as shape-shifting. Because they need air to breathe, they frequently swim to shore, shrug off their sealskins, and dance on the beach.

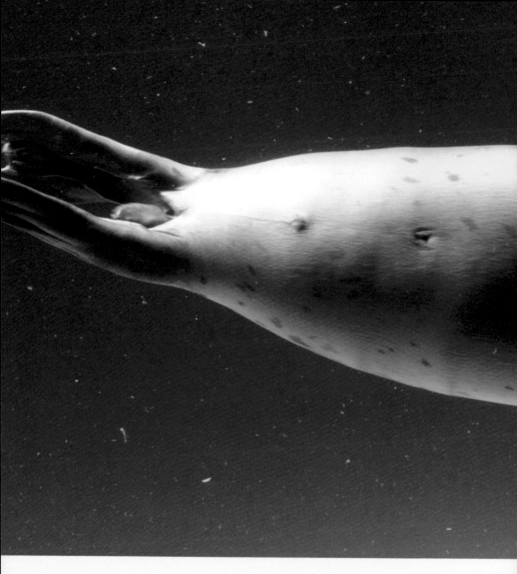

According to one legend, the first selkies were the children of the king of Lochlann. They and their offspring are forever cursed by a homesickness spell. When they are in the sea, they long for the land. When they are on land, they long to return to the sea. Many Scottish and Irish families claim to have "selkie blood." There are tales about

Sea creatures called selkies are thought to be able to change from seals into human form when they arrive on land.

members of the MacCodrum clan, who are seals in the daytime and humans at night. It is said that no member of the clan will ever hunt or kill a seal.

Ancient stories of seal-maidens forced to live on land with human husbands are numerous. As long as the men kept the seal skins safely hidden, their selkie wives were faithful and true. But if the seal-wives discovered their hidden skins, the selkies quickly abandoned their husbands and children and returned to the sea with an eager splash.

Mermaid Brides

In some tales told about them, mermaids are more unhappy than dangerous. They long for human souls. They want to go to heaven when they die. But the only way for a mermaid to gain a soul is to marry a human husband. There are many stories about these odd marriages. According to some, mermaids—like selkies—make wonderful wives. They are good cooks and loving mothers, who occasionally give birth to human children with webbed fingers and toes!

However, marrying a mermaid bride had its difficulties. And sadly, some of the marriages were ill-fated from the start. In Africa, there is a story about a mami wata who readily agreed to marry the love-struck young man who discovered her in the river. She reminded him, however, that she must never become completely dry. The young man was so eager to show his new bride to his parents that he forgot to bring water on their trip to the parents' home. The farther and farther away the mermaid traveled from the river, the more wilted she became. Finally, she shriveled up and died. Her forgetful new husband was heartbroken.

 Mermaids

The sea sprite Undine married her unsuspecting husband, Sir Huldbrand (left), in Friedrich de la Motte Fouqué's tale, Undine.

This Undine fountain (right) is located in Austria. After her husband is buried, Undine is transformed from a mermaid into a fountain.

Undine, a book by Baron Friedrich de la Motte Fouqué, published in 1811, relates the tale of a feisty sea sprite raised by a fisherman and his wife. Undine grows up to marry a handsome German knight named Sir Huldbrand. The knight is dismayed when he learns that his wife is not human and curses her. Undine kills her husband with a kiss and later terrorizes those at his funeral. When her husband is buried, she dissolves into a flowing white fountain. The story of Undine has been re-told as both a ballet and an opera.

Perhaps the most famous tale about a mermaid bride is the medieval French legend of Melusina, the water-fay or freshwater mermaid. This story has been translated into many different languages. Many Europeans have claimed to be descendants of Melusina, who won the heart of a noble knight named Raymond. Melusina agreed to marry him, but only on the condition that she could spend each Saturday in absolute privacy so she could resume her mermaid form and lounge in a tub of water. Raymond agreed. Melusina gave birth to several children, but all were disfigured or deformed. One day, Raymond peeked into his wife's room through the keyhole. He saw Melusina lounging in the bath-tub and was shocked to see that her long slender legs had been transformed into a glossy blue and white fish tail! When Melusina heard Raymond's horrified cry, she leapt like a porpoise out of the bathroom window and disappeared.

CHAPTER 3

INVESTIGATING MERMAIDS

At one time, the existence of mermaids was considered to be true. Famous people like Sir Walter Raleigh and Captain John Smith believed them to be real. Many physicians, priests, and well-traveled diplomats and ambassadors also believed mermaids existed. Interestingly enough, people realized that there was a difference between the mermaids in folktales and legends and the ones that were reported by fisherman, sailors, and sea travelers. Most accounts of mermaid encounters have proven to be nothing more than tall tales. But there have been credible witnesses as well.

Eyewitness Accounts

In 1492 Christopher Columbus recorded in his captain's log that one of his seamen reported seeing a mermaid near the ship. He wrote down the description of the creature, declaring that it was "not so beautiful as they are painted, though to some extent they have a human appearance about the face."[2]

Explorer Henry Hudson, in 1608, also reported a mermaid sighting at sea: "From the navel upward, her back and breasts were like a woman's (as they say that saw her) her body as big as one of ours: her skin very white and long hair hanging down behind, the color black; in her going down they saw her tail which was like the tail of a porpoise and speckled like a mackerel. Their names that saw her were Thomas Hilles and Robert Raynar."[3]

In 1560 several Jesuit priests and the viceroy were asked to identify strange creatures caught in a net off the coast of

Christopher Columbus described the mermaids he supposedly encountered as not as beautiful as they were in paintings and some were even frightening.

Ceylon. All agreed that the odd marine animals were certainly merfolk of some sort. In 1820 the *American Journal of Science* carried an article relating an unusual entry in a ship captain's log. The captain of the *Leonidas* noted that on a recent voyage between New York and France, the passengers and crew observed a strange fish, nearly 5 feet (1.5m) long and resembling a human female from the waist up, swimming alongside the ship most of the afternoon. Everyone onboard had plenty of time to observe the unidentified creature and guessed it to be a mermaid.

Do Mermaids Exist?

In the 1st century A.D., Pliny the Elder stated in his huge book, *Natural History*, that mermaids did indeed exist. In 1717 an illustration of the Amboina mermaid was published in several science books. It had brown skin and a long blue tail. The caption described the mermaid as "a monster . . . caught near the island of Borne in the Department of Amboine. It was 59 inches [149.9cm] long and in proportion as an eel. It lived on land for four days and seven hours in a vat full of water. From time to time it uttered little cries like those of a mouse. Although offered small fish, shells, crabs and lobsters, etc., it would not eat. After its death some excreta, like that of a cat, was found in the barrel."[4]

But are mermaids real? That's what skeptics in the Danish government set out to discover when

The. Merman warns Banvilda in vain.

Like mermaids, it has not been proven that mermen exist.

they launched the first official investigation in 1723. When members of the Danish Royal Commission sighted a merman near the Faeroe Islands, they were astonished. The creature sank into the water as the Danish ship neared. Then it rose again to stare intently with deep-set eyes at those leaning over the ship's rail. According to the account, the merman puffed out his cheeks and roared before diving back into the waves.

In 1762 two French girls killed a mermaid on the beach while they were out searching for shells. A physician later examined the corpse. Both the incident and the doctor's description of the mermaid's body were reported in the local newspaper. The creature was described as having white skin, the breasts of a woman, a flat nose, a large mouth, a hairy chin, and the tail of a fish.

MERMAID OR MARINE ANIMAL?

Scientists today insist that there are no such things as mermaids, even though occasional mermaid sightings are still reported. Some scientists believe that these mermaid sightings can be attributed to mistaken identity or optical illusion.

Many people believe that marine creatures called **manatees** or **dugongs** are frequently mistaken for mermaids. Perhaps lonely sailors, missing their wives and sweethearts while on long sea voyages, thought these "sea cows," were women. These mammals often lean on rocks in the water while

Some scientists believe that instead of mermaids people are really seeing dugongs like the one pictured here.

nursing and cradle their young with their flippers. From a distance, they might resemble women with fish tails. Others insist that curious mermaids seen by seamen were nothing more than seals with long-lashed brown eyes.

 Mermaids

Some scientists say that the weather can play tricks on our eyes. Mist, fog, and other atmospheric conditions can cause sailors to mistake walruses for mermen. Air and light conditions can cause mirages or other optical illusions.

PRANKS, HOAXES, AND PRACTICAL JOKES

Another explanation is that some witnesses may see someone pretending to be a mermaid. One prankster in Cornwall in 1820 put on a seaweed wig and wrapped his legs in oilcloth. For several moonlit nights, he sat on a rock in the bay singing "God Save the King." Local villagers were enthralled at what they thought was a real mermaid. The villagers felt a bit foolish when they learned a short time later that it was nothing more than a student prank.

In the mid-1800s, Japanese fisherman used to sew monkey corpses and fish parts together. They sold these "stuffed mermaids" to gullible seamen and tourists. Soon, it was a popular fad. Everyone wanted to own a stuffed mermaid! Others were willing to pay to see **"embalmed"** and stuffed mermaid exhibits. Following the deadly tsunami in the Pacific Ocean in December 2004, photographs of fake "dead mermaids" that had washed up on beaches were circulated over the Internet.

Perhaps the most famous hoax of all is the "Feejee mermaid." American **entrepreneur** P. T. Barnum brought it to New York from London in

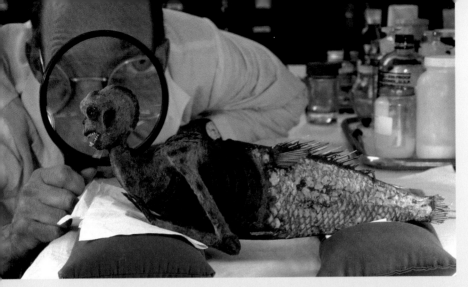

Scientists often find that items such as this mermaid skeleton are often revealed to be fakes after further investigation.

1842. It was an ugly manmade monstrosity with a monkey's head, a paper-mache tail, and the torso of a baby orangutan. Records indicate that Barnum tripled his museum income during the first month that the monstrosity was on display.

THE UNEXPLAINED

There is an odd, unexplained matter concerning mermaid sightings, however. Most descriptions provided by credible eyewitnesses do not match the descriptions of fairytale mermaids. They don't sing or talk. They don't have long golden hair and combs. They don't turn into women with legs on dry land. And oddly enough, most of the unexplained sightings occur in regions where manatees and other sea cows are not known to exist.

Cryptozoologists suggest that these creatures may be an unidentified species of marine life—perhaps even a **primate**—that has adapted to life in the water. But because no bodies have washed up on shore, no scientific studies have been launched. In the 1970s, natives on an island province of Papau New Guinea told an **anthropologist** about sea creatures called ri (pronounced ree). The ri were described as having long, dark bodies with a pair of fins instead of legs. The natives told the anthropologist that ri reminded them of the mermaids on tuna fish cans, but that these creatures did not seem to be intelligent.

It is unknown whether the natives were describing an unknown species of dugong, or if *ri* are something completely different. The elusive mermaid has been celebrated for centuries in myths, legends, and folktales. Following the public's fascination with stuffed mermaid exhibits, mermaids became popular subjects for stories, songs, and ballets. There were dishes, furniture, and even wallpaper created with mermaids on them. Mermaids have also been depicted on coins, medals, and postage stamps.

An 18th-century illustration of a "mere-maid," the African version of a mermaid. This African version is believed to be derived from primates.

CHAPTER 4

MERMAIDS EVERYWHERE!

During the late 1800s and early 1900s, famous artists like Herbert Draper and John William Waterhouse painted beautiful mermaids for art exhibits. Ballets with elaborate underwater scenes, like *Undine*, were popular. James Barrie's beautiful Mermaid Lagoon scene in his play *Peter Pan* delighted London theatergoers of the day.

STORYBOOK MERMAIDS

It was during this time that mermaids were transformed from deadly sea monsters into entertaining storybook subjects suitable for children. In 1863 Charles Kingsley's, *The Water Babies*, was a popular story about a little chimney sweep's underwater adventure with friendly merfolk.

In 1965 the children's book *The Animal Family* by Randall Jarell became a Newbery Honor Book. It tells the story of a lonely hunter who wins the trust of a mermaid, who speaks to him "in a voice like the water." He wants to take her home and describes his house as "a big wooden thing . . . that you stay inside at night or when it rains."

"Why?" the mermaid asks.

"To keep from getting wet," the hunter replies.

"To keep from getting *wet?*" the mermaid says despairingly.

Together, they adopt a bear cub and a lynx and a little boy. They all live happily in the woods.

"THE LITTLE MERMAID"

Perhaps the most famous fairytale mermaid is the one created by the Danish writer, Hans Christian Andersen. *The Little Mermaid* was published in 1836. It's the heartbreaking story of a young mermaid who saves the life of a drowning prince. In an effort to win his love and obtain a human soul, she sacrifices her beautiful voice. However, the handsome prince marries another. In the end, the little mermaid refuses to take her revenge upon him, and she dies.

The tale was immediately popular with adults and children around the world. The heroine of the story was immortalized in a bronze statue sculpted

The heroine of Hans Christian Andersen's story The Little Mermaid *was immortalized in a bronze statue found in Denmark.*

by Edvard Eriksen. It sits overlooking the sea in the harbor in Copenhagen, Denmark.

In 1989 Disney turned Andersen's familiar fairy tale into a popular animated film. The mermaid is named Ariel, and the story has a happy ending.

Inspired by the success of the Disney film, the Japanese released a popular 26-episode cartoon in 1991 called *Ningyo Hime Marino no Boken* (*The Adventures of Mermaid Princess Marina*).

MOVIE STAR MERMAIDS

But Ariel was not the first mermaid to make it to the big screen. In 1948 a British film titled *Miranda* was released. It starred actress Glynis Johns as a beautiful Cornish mermaid, who drags a vacationing doctor into her underwater cave and threatens to keep him there forever unless he promises to take her to see London.

An American film starring William Powell and Ann Blyth, as a mermaid named Lenore, was also released in 1948. *Mr. Peabody and the Mermaid* is the story of a middle-aged man on vacation in the Caribbean, who snags a lovely mermaid in his fishing line and takes her home—much to the annoyance of his jealous wife!

Splash! is perhaps the most successful movie about a mermaid. It was directed by Ron Howard and released by Disney in 1984. It stars Tom Hanks and Daryl Hannah as the beautiful mermaid named Madison. When Allen Bauer, portrayed by Tom Hanks, is a little boy he is saved from drowning by a young mermaid. Years later, Allen is rescued again by the same mermaid. This time she falls in love with him. Madison, like many folkloric mermaids, can transform her tail into a pair of legs. She does

Tom Hanks and Daryl Hannah appear in an advertisement for the film Splash!, *one of the most popular movies ever made featuring a mermaid.*

so and makes her way to New York City in search of her true love. Allen falls in love with Madison too–without realizing that she's a mermaid. But Madison's time on land is limited, and Allen is faced with a painful decision. Will he stay in the city without Madison or give up life as he knows it to join the mermaid in her underwater realm?

Aquamarine is one of the most recent movies about a mermaid seeking love. Based on the book by Alice Hoffman, it is the story of two best friends, Claire (played by Emma Roberts) and Hailey (Jo-anna "JoJo" Levesque), who find a mermaid named Aquamarine (Sara Paxton) in the beach club swimming pool. The mermaid promises to grant them a wish if they help her win the love of a handsome lifeguard named Raymond (Jake McDorman). In the end, both the girls, and the mermaid learn valuable lessons about life, love, and friendship.

Many other movies have underwater mermaid scenes too. In *Harry Potter and the Goblet of Fire* (2005), Harry encounters some merfolk. In the movie *Hook* (1991), the alluring residents of Mermaid Lagoon help a grown-up Peter Pan (played by Robin Williams), breathe underwater.

MERMAIDS TODAY

Today, one can see mermaids in many different places. Disney's Ariel appears on everything from postage stamps to sunscreen bottles, beach towels, and party favors. Starbucks Coffee uses a mermaid

logo on its cups and napkins. The Chicken of the Sea tuna fish company uses a mermaid logo too. In the 1960s, the company had a commercial jingle: *"Ask any mermaid you happen to see. . . . What's the best tuna? Chicken of the Sea!"*

Several companies use mermaids for their logos, such as the Chicken of the Sea tuna fish company.

Coney Island's annual Mermaid Parade in New York City brings thousands of visitors to see merfolk of all sorts every summer. Each year different celebrities are crowned King Neptune and Queen Mermaid to rule over the parade and the Mermaid Ball that follows. There are colorful floats, and lots of people wearing sailor suits and sea dragon costumes. Others wear sequined bikinis, fishnet dresses, and mermaid tails made from colored plastic wrap.

For nearly 50 years, families have visited Weeki Wachee Springs (north of Tampa, Florida), the City of Live Mermaids. There, one can watch trained mermaids perform in a pool of natural spring water that is 16 feet (4.9m) deep. The marine theater is built into the spring. There is no tank or aquarium. The mermaids smile and swish their tails and drink RC Cola. Sometimes, they perform with fish, turtles, manatees, and even the occasional Florida alligator!

For thousands of years, the elusive mermaid has captured the imagination of people around the world. She continues to do so in art, stories, and movies. But beware! With their hot tempers and boa-constrictor embrace, mermaids can be dangerous!

Mermaids perform at Weeki Wachee Springs, north of Tampa, Florida.

 Mermaids

NOTES

CHAPTER ONE: SAILOR, BEWARE!

1. Quoted in Beatrice Phillpotts, *Mermaids*. New York: Ballantine, 1980, p. 22.

CHAPTER THREE: INVESTIGATING MERMAIDS

2. Quoted in Caroll B. Fleming, "Maidens of the Sea Can Be Alluring, But Sailor, Beware!" *Smithsonian*, June 1983, p. 89.
3. Quoted in Gwen Benwell and Arthur Waugh, *Sea Enchantress*. New York: Citadel Press, 1965, p. 95.
4. Quoted in Benwell and Waugh, *Sea Enchantress*. p. 103.

GLOSSARY

anthropologist: One who studies the origins, behavior, and ethnic culture of humans.

cryptozoologists: People who study unknown or mythical creatures.

embalmed: A corpse that is protected from decay with preservatives.

entrepreneur: One who organizes and operates a business venture.

fertility: Being fertile or able to reproduce offspring.

flukes: The two divisions of a whale or dolphin's tail.

dugongs: Plant-eating, aquatic mammals native to tropical coastal waters.

manatees: Plant-eating, aquatic mammals.

logo: A sign, name, or trademark, often used in advertising.

metamorphosis: Changing shape, often by magic or sorcery.

omen: A sign or occurrence that foretells good or evil.

primate: Any creature with hands for grasping, such as monkeys, apes, and humans.

FOR FURTHER EXPLORATION

BOOKS

Jerome Clark, *Unexplained!* Canton, MI: Visible Ink Press, 1999. A fascinating reference book that compiles the strange and unexplained sightings of mermaids, the Loch Ness monster, and other cryptozoological creatures.

Georgess McHargue, *The Impossible People.* New York: Holt, Rinehart and Winston, 1972. An interesting look at the origins of mythological creatures such as mermaids, giants, and trolls.

Mary Pope Osborne, *Mermaid Tales from Around the World.* New York: Scholastic, 1972. A lively retelling of a dozen mermaid legends from different cultures around the globe.

Beatrice Phillpotts, *Mermaids.* New York: Ballantine Books, 1980. A historical overview of the mermaid and her transformation from monster to movie star. Includes many fine full-color illustrations.

WEB SITES

Humanity.org (www.humanity.org/voices/folklore/mermaids). This site offers an index of mermaid tales collected from around the world.

Mysterious Britain (www.mysteriousbri tain.co.uk/ folklore/mermaids.html). Lots of information on mermaids and folktales about them from Scotland, Wales, and England.

Weeki Wachee Springs–The City of Live Mermaids (www.mermaid.weekiwachee.com). This site offers photos of performing mermaids and provides their performance schedule at the popular Florida tourist site.

INDEX

PICTURE CREDITS

Cover: photos.com

Kelvin Aitken/Bruce Coleman, Inc. Reproduced by permission. 28

© Antman Archives/The Image Works, 24

The Art Archive/Private Collection/Marc Charmet, 8, 21 (above)

© Frank Blackburn/Dorling Kindersley/Getty Images, 18–19

© Tim Boyle/Getty Images News/Getty Images, 37

Stuart Dee/ Photographer's Choice/Getty Images, 34

© Mary Evans Picture Library/ The Image Works, 7, 9, 11

© Kevin Fleming/Corbis, 30

Illustration by H.J. Ford. © 2003 Charles Walker/Topfoto/The Image Works, 26

© Hulton-Deutsch Collection/ Corbis, 31

© Douglas Kirkland/Corbis, 35

© Erich Lessing/Art Resource, NY, 15, 21

The Mermaid (oil on canvas), Padday, Charles (1889-1947) / Private Collection, Photo © Bonhams, London, UK / The Bridgeman Art Library International. All rights reserved. Reproduced by permission. 5

© Réunion des Musées Nationaux/Art Resource, NY, 16

Robert Sullivan/AFP/Getty Images, 38

ABOUT THE AUTHOR

Shirley Raye Redmond is the author of several nonfiction books for children, including *The Dog That Dug for Dinosaurs*, *Tentacles! Tales of the Giant Squid*, and *Patriots in Petticoats: Heroines of the American Revolution*. Redmond lives in New Mexico. Visit her Web site at www.readshirleyraye.com.